SPARKING MEMORIES

Poetry by Gary Mex Glazner

Books
Poetry Slam: The Competitive Art of Performance Poetry,
Manic D Press, Editor
Ears on Fire: Snapshot Essays in a World of Poets, La Alameda Press
How to Make a Living as a Poet, Soft Skull Press

Fine Printing, Broadsides
Word Art: Poetry Broadside Series,
The Press at the Palace of the Governors, Editor

CDs
Fast as Knives
You Say You Are a Poet but even Your Wife Doesn't Believe You
¡PoetMan! Poetry for Children

Film
Busload of Poets, Director, Executive Producer

alzpoetry.com
www.poetryslam.com
poetmex@aol.com

Sparking Memories

THE ALZHEIMER'S POETRY PROJECT

ANTHOLOGY

EDITED BY

Gary Mex Glazner

POEM FACTORY   SANTA FE

ACKNOWLEDGMENTS

First and foremost to the patients and families I have worked with—
I am indebted to you for allowing me into your lives
to share my love of poetry.
I hope this book is of use to you.
Gratitude to the board of New Mexico Literary Arts
for their belief in the Alzheimer's Poetry Project (APP).
Thanks to J.B. Bryan for his guidance.
Thanks to Logan Phillips for his design help.
Without Ruth Dennis and her love of being a caregiver
the APP would not have gotten off to a strong start.
Thanks to Paul Ingles of "Good Radio"
for his fine sense of narrative and story.
Thanks to Lynn Cline for her coverage of poetry for many years
and how she helps build the audience for poetry.
Thanks to Linda Werthiemer of NPR's "Weekend Edition."
Thanks to Amy Wasserstrom "Today" show producer.
This book was made possible with funding from
the good folks at "Bread for the Journey,"
for their support I am ever grateful.
Thanks to the Puffin Foundation, Santa Fe Arts Commission,
and the State of New Mexico Arts Commission.
for their support of the Alzheimer's Poetry Project.
Thanks to all the poets who have helped with the project.
Cover photographs by Daniel Barsotti.
Always special thanks to Margaret Victor for muse duties.

alzpoetry.com
Poem Factory
12 Highview Lane,
Santa Fe, NM 87508

WE ARE FORGET

We are the words we have forgotten.
We are shifting and pacing.
We wrote this poem?
It's a pretty poem.
Can you bake a cherry pie?
Never more, never more.
We have no horizon.
We don't recall washing or eating
or what you just said.
Ask me my name.
Ask me if I have children.
You are my daughter?
Light washing over us moment, moment.
You're a handsome man.
You're a pretty lady.
You have beautiful eyes.
Wash me, put me to bed clean,
hold me as I fall asleep.
Give me a kiss, brush my hair.
Our handwriting is beautiful
twists and loops of letters,
we can't remember our hands.
Our ears are wishful,
we can't remember our ears.
We can speak every language,
we can't remember our mouths.
We are porous.
We are the past.
We are forget.
                    —*Gary Mex Glazner*

This book is dedicated to the memory of Frankie Glazner

…the smell and taste of things remain poised a long time, like souls,
ready to remind us, waiting and hoping for their moment, amid the ruins
of all the rest; and bear unfaltering, in the tiny and almost impalpable drop
of their essence, the vast structure of recollection.

—MARCEL PROUST

CONTENTS

The Alzheimer's Poetry Project (APP) is a simple idea: to read classic poems to the patients that they might have learned as children. APP is not the type of poetry reading that takes place from a podium. We recite the poems directly to the folks, often holding their hands. It is not unusual for visitors to become emotionally moved when witnessing a reading session. The people we serve are often in late stages of Alzheimer's and sometimes have a hard time holding a conversation or in some cases even speaking, when you see and hear them respond to the poems by saying words and lines along with the poet, it can be quite moving.

MY BACKGROUND

In 1997, I received a small grant from Poets and Writers magazine to give a series of workshops at a senior drop-in center in Northern California. One fellow in the class had his head down not able to participate. I was reciting the Longfellow poem "The Arrow and the Song." When I said the line, "I shot an arrow in the air," he looked up and said "where it lands I know not where." For that moment he was able to reach back to some part of his psyche that was not damaged by the disease. It was one of many wonderful moments we experienced during the workshop and showed me the power of reading those classic poems— I was hooked.

In December of 2003, I put together a simple proposal for the APP for the non-profit New Mexico Literary Arts to start a similar program in Santa Fe, at Sierra Vista Assisted Retirement Community. It turned out that one of the board member's father was afflicted with the disease. In fact, almost everyone I talk to about this project has some personal connection to the disease. They voted to fund the seed money to start the project.

Whenever I speak about the APP one question always comes up: "Do you have a family member with Alzheimer's?" I do not, however I do have a personal connection to using these poems with a loved one. When I first began this project in 1997, my mother was in the last stages of terminal cancer. Through a combination of the drugs she was given to relieve the pain and the progression of the cancer she had grown unable to think and communicate clearly.

One day my father called to ask me to come over as my mother was having a particularly hard time. On arriving, I found her quite agitated. I had with me the poems from the Alzheimer's program and I began to read to her and soon she was calm. Then my father Billy and I began to recite a poem that she had teased him with when they were childhood sweethearts. My mother quite gently began to say the poem along with us, even laughing as she joined in:

> Oh, where have you been Billy boy, Billy boy,
> Oh, where have you been, charming Billy?
> I have been to seek a wife, she's the joy of my young life,
> She's a young thing and cannot leave her mother.
>
> Can she make a cherry pie, Billy boy, Billy boy,
> Can she make a cherry pie, charming Billy?
> She can make a cherry pie, quick's a cat can wink her eye,
> She's a young thing and cannot leave her mother.

It was one of her last moments of real clarity and a moment of playfulness that quite powerfully brought home to me how these poems could be of use to people.

THE HUMOR

This won't come as news to those of you who are caregivers, but many of the Alzheimer's patients I have encountered are surprisingly funny. One of the men I work with was an army Sergeant for 30 years, when I read a poem he doesn't like, such as a rap version of "The Raven," he gives me the thumbs down, when he approves he gives me a thumbs up. When I read a love poem he plays an imaginary "air" violin. Whenever I bring in flowers, there is a woman in the group, who holds a flower in her teeth and does a kind of flamenco happy dance. The first session at Sierra Vista I brought in an ice chest full of snow. I let them feel the snow and many wanted to taste it. I made snow balls and they began to throw them at me. As I caught and dodged the snowballs it struck me that working with this group was going to be rewarding in ways I had not expected.

Along with the humor you can experience in working with Alzheimer's patients, working with them can also break your heart. One of the best things about the APP is that it allows you to work with the patients at the level they are able to function. In the group at Sierra Vista one of the women is able to say the word "Macaroni," with me when I recite "Yankee Doodle." She mouths other sections along with me, much as someone singing along with the radio does and I feel like she is recognizing parts of poems. When she says "Macaroni," there is warmth in her voice that reinforces her personality and drives home how much is lost. There is a searching quality to the way the patients look at you that is similar to a child's gaze when learning about the world— then the patients look away, or more accurately they fade into a place where you can't reach them.

GOALS

The main goal of the program is to increase the quality of life for the Alzheimer's patients and caregivers. The immediate goal of the program is to help as many people as possible to begin reading poetry to people afflicted with Alzheimer's Disease and other dementia.

WHO IS THIS BOOK FOR?

The intended audience for the APP is Alzheimer's patients, healthcare professionals, caregivers and poets. I am happy to give informational talks to community groups and healthcare professionals. Feedback on needs of the community has been and will continue to be solicited, analyzed and used to tailor the program to the community. At all stages of the program input from healthcare professionals has been sought out and utilized. If you are a healthcare professional and would like more information on the APP or to give feedback on your experience working with Alzheimer's patients please contact me at the address listed below.

A FEW THOUGHTS ON READING AND RECITING POETRY IN PUBLIC

Holding people's attention with poetry is always challenging, perhaps even more so when your audience is afflicted with dementia. I like to have at least a few poems memorized so I can walk around freely and recite the poems. In performance poetry lingo this is called, "working the room." With the Alzheimer's patients, I approach them and reach out my hand, shaking, holding their hands or just touching them if they show interest in interacting with me.

I tell them it is great to see them. I smile and speak in a nice loud voice. If you know their names use their name when saying hello. "Hello, Imogene, it's great to see you, how are you today." If they answer, "Good," respond to them. If you don't know their names, you can ask and then repeat the name. If they don't reach out to take your hand, you might gently touch their knee. Often they will be sleeping, if so you can gently touch them and see if they wake up. Occasionally, they may have their eyes closed but still be listening and your touch may be welcome. You are letting them know you care about them and letting them know you are there for them, you have come to see them.

This is a good public speaking technique, but it is interesting to note how many people coming into a room full of Alzheimer's patients will be shy about approaching them. People especially when first working with Alzheimer's patients may be taken aback by their physical condition, by their some time lack of interest in their visitors, but the above description of warming up the room, will build interest, help to get their attention and set the stage for your interaction with them whatever program you are presenting.

Often at poetry readings someone will read in what is called the "poetry voice." It is a monotone, with slight lilt, each line ending in a questioning up turn. Although, there is nothing wrong in principle in sounding that way, the problem comes when the person reads poem after poem with exactly the same sound. Imagine going to hear a band and every song sounded the same, or a play where the actors performed every scene with the same intensity and voice. We wouldn't stand for it, yet many poets think it is perfectly fine to read all their poems, no matter the subject, exactly the same.

Try projecting some of the poems like a street corner seller from Elizabethan England, say a fish monger. How about sounding like a hotdog vendor from a baseball game? Think of how an auctioneer sounds or a flight attendant. How would a lover read a poem before a fireplace in full woo mode? Try on different regional accents. There is such a richness of voice in a New England fisherman's voice, a Southern Belle's mint julep, or a Texas rodeo twang.

The idea is to be playful in your reading; to use a variety of volumes and intensity; to listen to all the wonderful voices around you and bring them into your reading. You don't have to be a perfect mimic, just be aware of all the possible sounds the human voice can make, from a conspiratorial whisper to a parachutist's falling shout of joy; from cooing baby; to a football coach's gaming winning rage. Put a little passion in your voice.

If you have a few of the poems memorized you can clap along with a particularly rhythmic poem. I sometimes clap out the rhythm to Blake's "Tyger." You can more easily look up and make eye contact with your audience. You can move around the room and recite a section to each person. I jump up out of my chair and recite, "Tyger, tyger, burning bright. In the forest of the night," to each member of the group as I circle around the room. Most of all I try to have fun with each poem.

In the reading sessions I alternate between a high energy rhythmic poem with hand holding and physical contact, a poignant poem with emphasis on the words, reading in a slower more sensuous voice and a funny poem, jazzed up with funny voices for about 30 minutes. I constantly appraise their individual reactions and the overall energy of the room and make subtle shifts in my recitation. I stop and respond when people speak to me incorporating their comments into the recitation of the poem and the flow of the program. I end on a high energy poem, often going back to the poem I started the program with. Once the reading of the poems is over, I once again go around and speak to each person, now thanking them for allowing me to come and spend time with them and for allowing me to share my love of poetry.

CONCLUSION

All the profits from the sale of this anthology go directly to the APP programming. When you purchase this book, you are contributing directly to poems being read to patients at assisted living centers.

Please contact me at the address listed below if you are interested in starting an APP in your community or if you just want to let me know how the book has worked for you. Feel free to offer feedback and suggestions. Please wish me luck with the Alzheimer's Poetry Project.

Gary Mex Glazner
Director, Alzheimer's Poetry Project
12 Highview Lane
Santa Fe, NM 87508
poetmex@aol.com
alzpoetry.com

Ruth Dennis has been the Recreational Director at Sierra Vista Retirement Community, Santa Fe, New Mexico for the past five years. She has an MFA from Cranbrook Academy of Art and an MA in Art Therapy from Southwestern College. She teaches classes on working with Alzheimer's patients at Southwestern College. Dennis has given creativity workshops at the New Mexico State Conference on Aging. She provides staff training for Open Hands. Dennis was an Artist-in-Residence at the Bemis Foundation. She has lived in Santa Fe for seven years. This is her first published article.

Dementia can be defined as a progressive, relentless forgetting, as a loss of one's existence as a person, continuing until death. I choose not to accept this definition. Remembrance and gain are also parts of this process. Memories that have been hidden by the day to day practical concerns become important again. A childhood rhyme, a certain set of musical notes, colors next to one another, the smell of green tomatoes, an attractive person that smiles when you flirt with them, these are the kind of memories that matter.

These memories become remembered again in dementia. That does not take away the fact that the disease process is frightening but it does help make the process more bearable. In dementia someone can gain entrance to places inside themselves that were put aside to hold a job, raise a family, and function in our world. These places offer an escape from the relentless loss of these diseases. In these rhymes, notes, smells and smiles one can forget about things like; confusion, incontinence, medicines that make one feel tired or nauseous, and confinement. They give one freedom, confidence, and laughter.

I am the Recreational Director at Sierra Vista Retirement Community, a fifteen bed Alzheimer's residence in Santa Fe, NM. Like most of my peers I have been trained in a culture that expects to see accomplishments, a skill should be learned, a therapeutic goal should be met, and progress should be made. The only progress in dementia care is to make the process more bearable. There is no linear improvement. No conscious resolution of anything. There are simply human beings living in the presence and often being controlled by something that is bigger than themselves. There is much medical understanding of how the process works, where the damage starts in the brain, the neurological processes that happen as these diseases progress, certain chemical interventions that offer hope, but right now the process cannot be stopped for the vast majority of people facing dementing illnesses, including Alzheimer's Disease. Goals as such do not exist.

Everyday— sometimes every minute, a person will change in themselves and in their relationship to their illness. The only goal is to make as much of life as possible have meaning and be pleasurable.

This is the place that good, solid loving caregiving, balanced activities, and support for Arts programs comes in. Without the base of rested, loving, caregivers who are able to meet someone's basic needs in such a way that these needs cease to be the main issue of someone's life, and are experienced in love, no activity or Arts program will be able to provide pleasure or freedom in the best possible way. Caregiving is the root; other programs are the branches. These branches are critical for providing a balanced life in the face of dementia.

Dementia strips away life to the most essential features. What our culture defines as a successful life ceases to be important. Memories of a distant past, the presence of children and animals, music, sunshine, these things are important. Fifty years ago is far more important and far more real than what was for breakfast, the questionable fact that someone visited yesterday, or that exercise is at 10:00 and arts and crafts is at 1:30 on Fridays.

Time as a linear, controlled, rational thing ceases to exist. What emerges is a sense of time that is fluid, it is 1945 and yesterday and tomorrow all at once. The same mind that cannot remember when to go to the bathroom, or if food was served, can hold on to the words of a hit song from 1937, or an obscure line of poetry from a dull English class decades ago. Every moment exists and disappears into an almost Zen like now. During any day the world is both a familiar experience and a completely new one. Connections are made, lost and remade, and found again, continually inside the now of dementia. One of our residents greets everyone that she sees as if she remembers them as children. She is beyond time as I understand it, the past memory of being surrounded by children and seeing them grow into healthy strong adults is more real than living in a world that is often filled with strangers.

This fluidity of time is one reason that the Alzheimer's Poetry Project has been effective with our residents. Language is more than words. It is a moment in time that is held within a handful of words and a certain rhythm. It is all of the sensations that are connected to the memory that a set of words can bring into the now. All of the emotions connected to that time can awaken feelings in the present. Roles such as clowning at center stage, being a young woman during a first love, being the good student, or being the teacher can all be explored and then set aside for another set of words and memories.

Another benefit of this project is a renewed connection to words as expressive language. The language centers of the brain are often severely affected by the disease processes in many types of dementia. Words and objects become disconnected. Words and ideas or feelings can become separated. Words cease to be language, they cease to be meaningful. This can often lead too much frustration. Poems and song lyrics can allow someone to reconnect to words as a means of expression. Feelings and ideas can be shared through the words of others. These feelings or ideas would not find any expression in words if the person were left to attempt to put the words together for themselves. The task of connecting the right word with the right idea or feeling would simply be too overwhelming, and would not get done. Poetry and music both have the ability to make words meaningful again. This provides a bridge back to expression in language again.

Someone once asked me "Why bother?" My answer to that is why not bother? Why not try as hard as possible to make the end of people's lives have beauty, humor and meaning? Why not continue to encourage creative expression in the face of devastating illness? The call to care for an aging population does not end in a research lab or a wellness center. It does not stop with a budget deficit. It continues through the individual lives that are lived out in the process of aging. For many people, that process includes diseases such as Alzheimer's that take away so many pieces of life. Why not do everything possible to make the lives of these individuals as meaningful as possible?

The call to care includes a call to respect the efforts of caregivers in all forms. It is a call to understand just how important programs such as the Alzheimer's Poetry Project are in the lives of people struggling with dementia. Arts programs provide moments of freedom in the face of devastating illness. I am blessed to work in a community where there is some support for music, performance, and poetry programs. These programs are critical pieces of the lives of many people. They deserve ongoing respect and support.

Ruth Dennis, MFA, MA.
Recreational Director /Sierra Vista Retirement Community
Santa Fe, New Mexico

IMPROVING PHYSICAL AND MENTAL HEALTH:
The Role of Cultural Arts

Kristen Sorocco received her Ph.D. in clinical psychology from Oklahoma State University where she specialized in geropsychology and cultural diversity issues. Dr. Sorocco is an Assistant Professor of Research in the Donald W. Reynolds Department of Geriatrics at the University of Oklahoma Health Sciences Center. Her interest in working with older adults began when she conducted her undergraduate honors thesis on the positive social and cognitive effects intergenerational programs provide individuals with dementia. While working on this project she immensely enjoyed the stories her older participants shared during their involvement in the study. From that point in time she has been conducting research with older adults examining the impact of culture on the conceptualization of mental health disorders and the effectiveness of psychoeducational programs for dementia caregivers. Her current research focuses on the assessment of psychophysiological and psychosocial variables associated with caregiver stress and brief treatment interventions designed to reduce caregiver stress. When she is not conducting research, Dr. Sorocco writes poetry and participates in the local poetry scene.

The professional and family caregivers of individuals living with a dementia diagnosis, such as Alzheimer's disease, with whom I have worked, constantly seek to discover novel ways to enhance the care recipient's quality of life. Individuals suffering with dementia often maintain a connection with their long-term memories, allowing them to access early life experiences. Cultural arts, such as music, dance, painting, and poetry are often associated with early life experiences and therefore can be incorporated into activities designed to enhance quality of life of individuals with dementia. Activities involving the cultural arts are enjoyable for both the care recipient as well as the care provider. Additionally, engaging in activities involving the cultural arts appears to have positive benefits for our emotional and physical health.

Of all the cultural arts, the influence of music on our physical and emotional health has received the greatest amount of research attention. Historically, Greek philosophers were the first to formally suggest the possible influence music has on our physical and emotional health (Levman, 2000). Current day research indicates that the cultural arts, such as music, do indeed enhance positive emotions and improve immune functioning among healthy individuals (Kreutz, Bongard, Rohrmann, Hodapp, & Grebe, in press). The influence of music also appears to positively benefit individuals with dementia. Individuals with possible or probable Alzheimer's disease have been known to continue to play familiar songs skillfully, despite their dementias and in one reported case learn a new song, which was published after the onset of their dementia (Cowles et aal., 2003). Listening to music has been shown to improve visual-spatial task performance (Johnson, Shaw, Vuong, Vuong, & Cotman, 2002), reduce agitation (Jenning and Vance, 2002; Gerdner, 2000), decrease wandering (Fitzgerald-Cloutier, 1993), enhance positive social behavior (Pollack & Namazi, 1992), and improve quality of life (Aldridge, 1998; Lipe, 1991) among individuals with Alzheimer's disease. Given the apparent benefits of incorporating music into programs for individuals with dementia the role of music therapy is increasing in dementia respite care (Yaya Kelleher, 2001). Dance and art therapy exhibit similar benefits for individuals with dementia. Physical and emotional needs of individuals with late stage Alzheimer's disease have been met through dance sessions to old, familiar music (Milchrist, 2001). Involvement in an art program for individuals with dementing illnesses have been found to positively effect the individuals' sense of positive well-being (Rentz, 2002).

Poetry, although less studied, is another form of art that could be used to enhance the quality of life of individuals with dementia. Poetry as an art form shares similar traits with music in that it involves verbal communication recited in rhythmic pattern. Diagnostically, symptoms of behavioral problems often associated with dementia have been identified in poems and other forms of writing completed by individuals with a dementia diagnosis. The writings of Mervyn Peake (1922-1968) illustrate symptoms of paranoia experienced by some individuals with dementia as well as the breakdown of writing skills as his dementia progressed (Sahlas, 2003). In addition to serving as a diagnostic tool, poetry also can be used as a treatment intervention. The use of poetry with individuals suffering with dementia has helped to meet their spiritual needs (Richards, 1990), as well as improve group cohesion and social interaction (Silber and Hes, 1995). Given the research findings on the benefits of using music and poetry as activities for individuals living with dementia and their caregivers, I have no doubt all involved will enjoy the Alzheimer's Poetry Project. Observing a smile can make your day when you are caring for someone with dementia, may sharing poetry bring you many smiles.

Kristen H. Sorocco, Ph.D.
Assistant Professor of Research
Donald W. Reynolds Dept. of Geriatric Medicine
University of Oklahoma Health Sciences Center

REFERENCES

Aldridge, D., (1998). Music therapy and the treatment of Alzheimer's disease. Journal of Clinical Geropsychology, 4(1), 17-30.

Fitzgerald-Cloutier, M.L. (1993). The use of music therapy to decrease wandering: An alternative to restraints. Music Therapy Perspectives, 11(1), 32-36.

Gerdner, L.A. (2000). Effects of individualized versus classical "relaxation" music on the frequency of agitation in elderly persons with Alzheimer's disease and related disorders. International Psychogeriatrics, 12(1), 49-65.

Jennings, B. and Vance, D. (2002). The short-term effects of music therapy on different types of agitation in adults with Alzheimer's. Activities, Adaptation & Aging, 26(4), 27-33.

Johnson, J.K., Shaw, G.L., Vuong, M., Vuong, S., & Cotman, C.W. (2002). Short-term improvement on a visual-spatial task after music listening in Alzheimer's disease: A group study.

Kreutz, G., Bongard, S., Rohrmann, S., Hodapp, V., & Grebe, D. (In Press). Effects of choir singing or listening on secretory immunoglobulin A, cortisol, and emotional state. Journal of Behavioral Medicine.

Lipe, A.W. (1991). Using music therapy to enhance the quality of life in a client with Alzheimer's dementia: A case study. Music Therapy Perspectives, 9, 102-105.

Milchrist, P. (2001). Alzheimer's: Cultivating optimal levels of flow through dance. Journal of Aging & Physical Activity, 9(3), 265-268.

Pollack, N.J. and Namazi, K.H. (1992). The effect of music participation on the social behavior of Alzheimer's disease patients. Journal of Music

LILLIAN BASSMAN DANK'S RESPONSE TO "TIME TO RISE," BY ROBERT LOUIS STEVENSON

A BIRDIE with a yellow bill
Hopped upon the window sill,
Cocked his shining eye and said:
"Ain't you' shamed, you sleepy-head!"

One of the great things about the Alzheimer's Poetry Project are the people you meet and the stories you hear. Sandy Speier heard the NPR broadcast and arranged for me to work with several facilities in Denver including the one where her mom lives. Here is Sandy's piece about her mom's poem.

My mother, Lillian Bassman Dank, wrote this poem when she was in a middle stage of Alzheimer's Disease. I told her that I would read her Susanna's favorite poem, "A Birdie with a Yellow Bill." It was a poem that my mother had recited, by heart, to me when I was a little girl, and I, in turn, often recited it to my children, Suze and Alex. My Mom listened to the poem and then, on the spot, created the little verse that follows:

And there was another bird that stood
Upon its feet and looked for food,
And stood and looked and didn't say
Anything, but went away.

Is my Mom, in her mid-stage Alzheimer's disease, a little bird that is unable to chirp out even when she enjoys good moments--as when we share bits of food that date back to Mom's childhood in the Ukraine--yogurt, blueberries, cherries, challah. My mother still speaks about "going away" or "not being here." Or, am I like the silent little bird as I visit Mom and feel the pain of watching her decline into late stage Alzheimer's and her imminent death? I am always trying to encourage the Shalom Park nurses and activities staff to awaken the humanity of the late stage residents. I don't like to see the late-stagers parked in their wheelchairs and isolated from staff members and from each other. These souls should be hearing human voices, poetry, and music. I look for crumbs of attention from the staff, but often everyone is too busy to care for them. Before long, I walk away, too--like Mom's bird who stands and looks and doesn't say/anything but goes away.

—Sandy Speier

POEMS

Though I am old with wandering
Through hollow lands and hilly lands,
I will find out where she has gone,
And kiss her lips and take her hands;
And walk among long dappled grass,
And pluck till time and times are done
The silver apples of the moon,
The golden apples of the sun.

— William Butler Yeats

THE TYGER
    —William Blake

Tyger! Tyger! burning bright
In the forests of the night,
What immortal hand or eye
Could frame thy fearful symmetry?

In what distant deeps or skies
Burnt the fire of thine eyes?
On what wings dare he aspire?
What the hand dare seize the fire?

And what shoulder, & what art.
Could twist the sinews of thy heart?
And when thy heart began to beat,
What dread hand? & what dread feet?

What the hammer? What the chain?
In what furnace was thy brain?
What the anvil? What dread grasp
Dare its deadly terrors clasp?

When the stars threw down their spears,
And watered heaven with their tears,
Did he smile his work to see?
Did he who made the Lamb make thee?

Tyger! Tyger! burning bright
In the forests of the night,
What immortal hand or eye
Dare frame thy fearful symmetry?

SONNET 18
—William Shakespeare

Shall I compare thee to a summer's day?
Thou art more lovely and more temperate:
Rough winds do shake the darling buds of May,
And summer's lease hath all too short a date:
Sometime too hot the eye of heaven shines,
And often is his gold complexion dimm'd;
And every fair from fair sometime declines,
By chance or nature's changing course untrimm'd;
But thy eternal summer shall not fade
Nor lose possession of that fair thou owest;
Nor shall Death brag thou wander'st in his shade,
When in eternal lines to time thou growest:
So long as men can breathe or eyes can see,
So long lives this and this gives life to thee.

THE OWL AND THE PUSSY-CAT
   —Edward Lear

The Owl and the Pussy-Cat went to sea
   In a beautiful pea-green boat,
They took some honey, and plenty of money,
   Wrapped up in a five pound-note.
The Owl looked up to the stars above,
   And sang to a small guitar,
'O lovely Pussy! O Pussy, my love,
   What a beautiful Pussy you are,
      You are,
      You are!
   What a beautiful Pussy you are.'

Pussy said to the Owl, 'You elegant fowl,
   How charmingly sweet you sing.
O let us be married, too long have we tarried,
   But what shall we do for a ring?'
They sailed away for a year and a day,
   To the land where the Bong-tree grows,
And there in the wood a Piggy-wig stood,
   With a ring in the end of his nose,
      His nose,
      His nose!
   With a ring in the end of his nose.

'Dear Pig, are you willing, to sell for one shilling
   Your ring?' Said the Piggy, 'I will.'
So they took it away, and were married next day,
   By the Turkey who lives on the hill.
They dined on mince, and slices of quince,
   Which they ate with a runcible spoon;
And hand in hand, on the edge of the sand,
   They danced by the light of the moon,
      The moon,
      The moon!
   They danced by the light of the moon.

CHILDREN
     -Anonymous

Monday's child is fair of face,
Tuesday's child is full of grace,
Wednesday's child is full of woe,
Thursday's child has far of go,
Friday's child is loving and giving,
Saturday's child works hard for his living,
And the child that is born on the Sabbath day
Is bonny and blithe, and good and gay.

WYNKEN, BLYNKEN, AND NOD
—Eugene Field

Wynken, Blynken, and Nod one night
Sailed off in a wooden shoe---
Sailed on a river of crystal light,
Into a sea of dew.
"Where are you going, and what do you wish?"
The old moon asked the three.
"We have come to fish for the herring fish
That live in this beautiful sea;
Nets of silver and gold have we!"
Said Wynken,
Blynken,
And Nod.
The old moon laughed and sang a song,
As they rocked in the wooden shoe,
And the wind that sped them all night long
Ruffled the waves of dew.
The little stars were the herring fish
That lived in that beautiful sea---
"Now cast your nets wherever you wish---
Never afeard are we";
So cried the stars to the fishermen three:
Wynken,
Blynken,
And Nod.
All night long their nets they threw
To the stars in the twinkling foam---
Then down from the skies came the wooden shoe,
Bringing the fishermen home;
'T was all so pretty a sail it seemed
As if it could not be,
And some folks thought 't was a dream they 'd dreamed
Of sailing that beautiful sea---
But I shall name you the fishermen three:
Wynken,
Blynken,
And Nod.

Wynken and Blynken are two little eyes,
And Nod is a little head,
And the wooden shoe that sailed the skies
Is a wee one's trundle-bed.
So shut your eyes while mother sings
Of wonderful sights that be,
And you shall see the beautiful things
As you rock in the misty sea,
Where the old shoe rocked the fishermen three:
Wynken,
Blynken,
And Nod.

HOW DO I LOVE THEE?
   —Elizabeth Barrett Browning

How do I love thee? Let me count the ways.
I love thee to the depth and breadth and height
My soul can reach, when feeling out of sight
For the ends of being and ideal grace.
I love thee to the level of every day's
Most quiet need, by sun and candle-light.
I love thee freely, as men strive for right.
I love thee purely, as they turn from praise.
I love thee with the passion put to use
In my old griefs, and with my childhood's faith.
I love thee with a love I seemed to lose
With my lost saints. I love with the breath,
Smiles, tears, of all my life; and, if God choose,
I shall but love thee better after death.

BARTER

—Sara Teasdale

Life has loveliness to sell,
All beautiful and splendid things,
Blue waves whitened on a cliff,
Soaring fire that sways and sings,
And children's faces looking up,
Holding wonder like a cup.
Life has loveliness to sell,
Music like a curve of gold,
Scent of pine trees in the rain,
Eyes that love you, arms that hold,
And for your spirit's still delight,
Holy thoughts that star the night.
Spend all you have for loveliness,
Buy it and never count the cost;
For one white singing hour of peace
Count many a year of strife well lost,
And for a breath of ecstasy
Give all you have been, or could be.

PURPLE COW
    —Gelette Burgess

I never saw a purple cow,
I hope I never see one;
But I can tell you, anyhow,
I'd rather see then be one.

I've never seen a purple cow.
My eyes with tears are full.
I've never seen a purple cow,
And I'm a purple bull.

MY SHADOW

—Robert Louis Stevenson

I have a little shadow that goes in and out with me,
And what can be the use of him is more than I can see.
He is very, very like me from the heels up to the head;
And I see him jump before me, when I jump into my bed.

The funniest thing about him is the way he likes to grow--
Not at all like proper children, which is always very slow;
For he sometimes shoots up taller like an india-rubber ball,
And he sometimes goes so little that there's none of him at all.

He hasn't got a notion of how children ought to play,
And can only make a fool of me in every sort of way.
He stays so close behind me, he's a coward you can see;
I'd think shame to stick to nursie as that shadow sticks to me!

One morning, very early, before the sun was up,
I rose and found the shining dew on every buttercup;
But my lazy little shadow, like an arrant sleepy-head,
Had stayed at home behind me and was fast asleep in bed.

JABBERWOCKY
   —Lewis Carroll

`Twas brillig, and the slithy toves
Did gyre and gimble in the wabe:
All mimsy were the borogoves,
And the mome raths outgrabe.
"Beware the Jabberwock, my son!
The jaws that bite, the claws that catch!
Beware the Jubjub bird, and shun
The frumious Bandersnatch!"
He took his vorpal sword in hand:
Long time the manxome foe he sought --
So rested he by the Tumtum tree,
And stood awhile in thought.
And, as in uffish thought he stood,
The Jabberwock, with eyes of flame,
Came whiffling through the tulgey wood,
And burbled as it came!
One, two! One, two! And through and through
The vorpal blade went snicker-snack!
He left it dead, and with its head
He went galumphing back.
"And, has thou slain the Jabberwock?
Come to my arms, my beamish boy!
O frabjous day! Callooh! Callay!'
He chortled in his joy.
`Twas brillig, and the slithy toves
Did gyre and gimble in the wabe;
All mimsy were the borogoves,
And the mome raths outgrabe.

BED IN SUMMER
        —Robert Louis Stevenson

In winter I get up at night
And dress by yellow candle-light.
In summer, quite the other way,
I have to go to bed by day.

I have to go to bed and see
The birds still hopping on the tree,
Or hear the grown-up people's feet
Still going past me in the street.

And does it not seem hard to you,
When all the sky is clear and blue,
And I should like so much to play,
To have to go to bed by day?

DAFFODILS
   —William Wordsworth

I wandered lonely as a cloud
That floats on high over vales and hills,
When all at once I saw a crowd,
A host, of golden daffodils;
Beside the lake, beneath the tress,
Fluttering and dancing in the breeze.

Continuous as the stars that shine
And twinkle on the Milky Way,
They stretched in never-ending line
Along the margin of a bay;
Ten thousand saw I at a glance,
Tossing their heads in a sprightly dance,

The waves beside them danced, but they
Outdid the sparkling waves in glee.
A poet could not but be gay,
In such a jocund company!
I gazed, and gazed but little thought
What wealth the show to me had brought;

For oft, when on my couch I lie
In vacant or in pensive mood,
They flash upon that inward eye
Which is the bliss of solitude;
And then my heart with pleasure fills,
And dances with the daffodils.

SPRING

-William Shakespeare

When daffodils begin to peer,
With heigh! the doxy, over the dale,
Why, then come in the sweet o' the year;
For the red blood reigns in the winter's pale.

The white sheet bleaching on the hedge,
With heigh! the sweet birds, O, how they sing!
Doth set my pugging tooth on edge,
For a quart of ale is dish for a king.

The lark, that tirra-lirra chants,
With heigh! the thrush and the jay,
Are summer songs for me and my aunts,
While we lie tumbling in the hay.

O BLUSH NOT SO!
    —John Keats

O blush not so! O blush not so!
Or I shall think ye knowing;
And if you smile the blushing while
Then maidenheads are going.

There's a blush for want, and a blush for shan't
And a blush for having done it:
There's a blush for thought and a blush for naught
And a blush for just begun it.

There's a sigh for aye, and a sigh for nay,
And a sigh for I can't bear it!
O what can be done, shall we stay or run?
O cut the sweet apple and share it.

THE RAVEN
        —Edgar Allen Poe

Once upon a midnight dreary, while I pondered, weak and weary,
Over many a quaint and curious volume of forgotten lore,
While I nodded, nearly napping, suddenly there came a tapping,
As of some one gently rapping, rapping at my chamber door.
"'Tis some visitor," I muttered, "tapping at my chamber door-
Only this, and nothing more."

Ah, distinctly I remember it was in the bleak December,
And each separate dying ember wrought its ghost upon the floor.
Eagerly I wished the morrow;- vainly I had sought to borrow
From my books surcease of sorrow- sorrow for the lost Lenore-
For the rare and radiant maiden whom the angels name Lenore-
Nameless here for evermore.

And the silken sad uncertain rustling of each purple curtain
Thrilled me- filled me with fantastic terrors never felt before;
So that now, to still the beating of my heart, I stood repeating,
"'Tis some visitor entreating entrance at my chamber door-
Some late visitor entreating entrance at my chamber door;-
This it is, and nothing more."

Presently my soul grew stronger; hesitating then no longer,
"Sir," said I, "or Madam, truly your forgiveness I implore;
But the fact is I was napping, and so gently you came rapping,
And so faintly you came tapping, tapping at my chamber door,
That I scarce was sure I heard you"- here I opened wide the door;-
Darkness there, and nothing more.

Deep into that darkness peering, long I stood there wondering, fearing,
Doubting, dreaming dreams no mortals ever dared to dream before;
But the silence was unbroken, and the stillness gave no token,
And the only word there spoken was the whispered word, "Lenore!"
This I whispered, and an echo murmured back the word, "Lenore!"-
Merely this, and nothing more.

Back into the chamber turning, all my soul within me burning,
Soon again I heard a tapping somewhat louder than before.
"Surely," said I, "surely that is something at my window lattice:
Let me see, then, what thereat is, and this mystery explore-
Let my heart be still a moment and this mystery explore;-
'Tis the wind and nothing more."

Open here I flung the shutter, when, with many a flirt and flutter,
In there stepped a stately raven of the saintly days of yore;
Not the least obeisance made he; not a minute stopped or stayed he;
But, with mien of lord or lady, perched above my chamber door-
Perched upon a bust of Pallas just above my chamber door-
Perched, and sat, and nothing more.

Then this ebony bird beguiling my sad fancy into smiling,
By the grave and stern decorum of the countenance it wore.
"Though thy crest be shorn and shaven, thou," I said, "art sure no craven,
Ghastly grim and ancient raven wandering from the Nightly shore-
Tell me what thy lordly name is on the Night's Plutonian shore!"
Quoth the Raven, "Nevermore."

Much I marveled this ungainly fowl to hear discourse so plainly,
Though its answer little meaning- little relevancy bore;
For we cannot help agreeing that no living human being
Ever yet was blest with seeing bird above his chamber door-
Bird or beast upon the sculptured bust above his chamber door,
With such name as "Nevermore."

But the raven, sitting lonely on the placid bust, spoke only
That one word, as if his soul in that one word he did out pour.
Nothing further then he uttered- not a feather then he fluttered-
Till I scarcely more than muttered, "other friends have flown before-
On the morrow he will leave me, as my hopes have flown before."
Then the bird said, "Nevermore."

Startled at the stillness broken by reply so aptly spoken,
"Doubtless," said I, "what it utters is its only stock and store,
Caught from some unhappy master whom unmerciful Disaster
Followed fast and followed faster till his songs one burden bore-
Till the dirges of his Hope that melancholy burden bore
Of 'Never- nevermore'."

But the Raven still beguiling all my fancy into smiling,
Straight I wheeled a cushioned seat in front of bird, and bust and door;
Then upon the velvet sinking, I betook myself to linking
Fancy unto fancy, thinking what this ominous bird of yore-
What this grim, ungainly, ghastly, gaunt and ominous bird of yore
Meant in croaking "Nevermore."

This I sat engaged in guessing, but no syllable expressing
To the fowl whose fiery eyes now burned into my bosom's core;
This and more I sat divining, with my head at ease reclining
On the cushion's velvet lining that the lamp light gloated o'er,
But whose velvet violet lining with the lamp light gloating o'er,
She shall press, ah, nevermore!

Then me thought the air grew denser, perfumed from an unseen censer
Swung by Seraphim whose footfalls tinkled on the tufted floor.
"Wretch," I cried, "thy God hath lent thee- by these angels he hath sent
thee
Respite- respite and nepenthe, from thy memories of Lenore!
Quaff, oh quaff this kind nepenthe and forget this lost Lenore!"
Quoth the Raven, "Nevermore."

"Prophet!" said I, "thing of evil!- prophet still, if bird or devil!-
Whether Tempter sent, or whether tempest tossed thee here ashore,
Desolate yet all undaunted, on this desert land enchanted-
On this home by horror haunted- tell me truly, I implore-
Is there- is there balm in Gilead?- tell me- tell me, I implore!"
Quoth the Raven, "Nevermore."

"Prophet!" said I, "thing of evil- prophet still, if bird or devil!
By that Heaven that bends above us- by that God we both adore-
Tell this soul with sorrow laden if, within the distant Aidenn,
It shall clasp a sainted maiden whom the angels name Lenore-
Clasp a rare and radiant maiden whom the angels name Lenore."
Quoth the Raven, "Nevermore."

"Be that word our sign in parting, bird or fiend," I shrieked, upstarting-
"Get thee back into the tempest and the Night's Plutonian shore!
Leave no black plume as a token of that lie thy soul hath spoken!
Leave my loneliness unbroken!- quit the bust above my door!
Quoth the Raven, "Nevermore."

And the Raven, never flitting, still is sitting, still is sitting
On the pallid bust of Pallas just above my chamber door;
And his eyes have all the seeming of a demon's that is dreaming,
And the lamp light o'er him streaming throws his shadow on the floor;
And my soul from out that shadow that lies floating on the floor
Shall be lifted- nevermore!

FIRST TIME HE KISSED ME
—Elizabeth Barrett Browning

I thought once how Theocritus had sung
But only three in all God's universe
Unlike are we, unlike, O princely Heart!
Thou hast thy calling to some palace-floor
I lift my heavy heart up solemnly
Go from me. Yet I feel that I shall stand
 The face of all the world is changed, I think
What can I give thee back, O liberal
 Can it be right to give what I can give?
Yet, love, mere love, is beautiful indeed
 And therefore if to love can be desert
 Indeed this very love which is my boast
 And wilt thou have me fashion into speech
 If thou must love me, let it be for nought
Accuse me not, beseech thee, that I wear
And yet, because thou overcomest so
My poet thou canst touch on all the notes
I never gave a lock of hair away
The soul's Rialto hath its merchandize
Beloved, my beloved, when I think
Say over again, and yet once over again
When our two souls stand up erect and strong
Is it indeed so? If I lay here dead
Let the world's sharpness like a clasping knife
A heavy heart, Beloved, have I borne
I lived with visions for my company
My own Beloved, who hast lifted me
My letters! all dead paper, mute and white!
I think of thee!--my thoughts do twine and bud
I see thine image through my tears to-night
Thou comest! all is said without a word
The first time that the sun rose on thine oath
Yes, call me by my pet-name! let me hear
With the same heart, I said, I'll answer thee
If I leave all for thee, wilt thou exchange

When we met first and loved, I did not build
Pardon, oh, pardon, that my soul should make
First time he kissed me, he but only kissed
Because thou hast the power and own'st the grace
Oh, yes! they love through all this world of ours!
I thank all who have loved me in their hearts
My future will not copy fair my past
How do I love thee? Let me count the ways
Beloved, thou hast brought me many flowers

DOUBLE, DOUBLE TOIL AND TROUBLE
Macbeth Act 4, Scene 1
       — William Shakespeare

A dark Cave. In the middle, a Caldron boiling. Thunder. Enter the three
Witches.

1 WITCH. Thrice the brindled cat hath mew'd.
2 WITCH. Thrice and once, the hedge-pig whin'd.
3 WITCH. Harpier cries:—'tis time! 'tis time!
1 WITCH. Round about the caldron go;
In the poison'd entrails throw.—
Toad, that under cold stone,
Days and nights has thirty-one;
Swelter'd venom sleeping got,
Boil thou first i' the charmed pot!
ALL. Double, double toil and trouble;
Fire burn, and caldron bubble.
2 WITCH. Fillet of a fenny snake,
In the caldron boil and bake;
Eye of newt, and toe of frog,
Wool of bat, and tongue of dog,
Adder's fork, and blind-worm's sting,
Lizard's leg, and owlet's wing,—
For a charm of powerful trouble,
Like a hell-broth boil and bubble.
ALL. Double, double toil and trouble;
Fire burn, and caldron bubble.
3 WITCH. Scale of dragon; tooth of wolf;
Witches' mummy; maw and gulf
Of the ravin'd salt-sea shark;
Root of hemlock digg'd i the dark;
Liver of blaspheming Jew;
Gall of goat, and slips of yew
Sliver'd in the moon's eclipse;
Nose of Turk, and Tartar's lips;
Finger of birth-strangled babe
Ditch-deliver'd by a drab,—

Make the gruel thick and slab:
Add thereto a tiger's cauldron,
For the ingredients of our caldron.
Finger of birth-strangled babe
Ditch-deliver'd by a drab,—
Make the gruel thick and slab:
Add thereto a tiger's cauldron,
For the ingredients of our caldron.
ALL. Double, double toil and trouble;
Fire burn, and caldron bubble.

THE ARROW AND THE SONG
        —Henry Wadsworth Longfellow

I shot an arrow into the air,
It fell to earth, I knew not where;
For, so swiftly it flew, the sight
Could not follow it in its flight.

I breathed a song into the air,
It fell to earth, I knew not where;
For who has sight so keen and strong,
That it can follow the flight of song?

Long, long afterward, in an oak
I found the arrow, still unbroke;
And the song, form beginning to end,
I found again in the heart of a friend.

A DREAM WITHIN A DREAM
   —Edgar Allen Poe

Take this kiss upon thy brow!
And, in parting from you now,
Thus much let me avow—
You are not wrong, to deem
That my days have been a dream;
Yet if hope has flown away
In a night, or in a day,
In a vision, or in none,
Is it therefore the less gone?
All that we see or seem
Is but a dream within a dream.
I stand amid the roar
Of a surf-tormented shore,
And I hold within my hand
Grains of the golden sand—
How few! yet how they creep
Through my fingers to the deep,
While I weep—while I weep!
O God! can I not grasp
Them with a tighter clasp?
O God! can I not save
One from the pitiless wave?
Is all that we see or seem
But a dream within a dream?

ROCK ME TO SLEEP
        —Elizabeth Akers Allen

Backward, turn backward, O Time, in your flight,
Make me a child again just for to-night!
Mother, come back from the echoless shore,
Take me again to your heart as of yore;
Kiss from my forehead the furrows of care,
Smooth the few silver threads out of my hair;
Over my slumbers your loving watch keep—
Rock me to sleep mother—rock me to sleep!

Backward, flow backward, O tide of the years!
I am so weary of toil and of tears—
Toil without recompense, tears all in vain—
Take them and give me my childhood again!
I have grown weary of dust and decay,
Weary of sowing for others to reap—
Rock me to sleep mother—rock me to sleep!

Mother, dear mother, the years have been long
Since I last listened your lullaby song;
Sing, then and unto my soul it shall seem
Womanhood's years have been only a dream.
Clasped to your heart in a loving embrace,
With your light lashes just sweeping my face,
Never hereafter to wake or to weep—
Rock me to sleep mother—rock me to sleep!

ANSWER TO A CHILD'S QUESTION
      —Samuel Taylor Coleridge

Do you ask what the birds say? The sparrow, the dove,
The linner and thrush say, "I love and I love!"
In the winter they're silent - the wind is so strong;
What is says, I don't know, but it sings a loud song.
But green leaves, and blossoms, and sunny warm weather,
And singing, and loving - all come back together.
But the lark is so brimful of gladness and love,
The green fields below him, the blue sky above,
That he sings, and he sings; and for ever sings he-
"I love my Love, and my Love loves me!"

SHE WALKS IN BEAUTY
    —Lord Byron

She walks in beauty, like the night
Of cloudless climes and starry skies;
And all that's best of dark and bright
Meet in her aspect and her eyes:
Thus mellow'd to that tender light
Which heaven to gaudy day denies.

One shade the more, one ray the less,
Had half impair'd the nameless grace
Which waves in every raven tress,
Or softly lighten o'er her face;
Where thoughts serenely sweet express
How pure, how dear their dwelling-place.

And on that cheek, and o'er that brow,
So soft, so calm, yet eloquent,
The smiles that win, the tints that glow,
But tell of days in goodness spent,
A mind at peace with all below,
A heart whose love is innocent!

A RED, RED ROSE
    —Robert Burns

O my Luve's like a red, red rose
That's newly sprung in June:
O my Luve's like the melodie
That's sweetly play'd in tune!
As fair thou art, my bonnie lass,
So deep in love am I:
And I will love thee still, my dear,
Till a' the seas gang dry:
Till a' the seas gang dry, my dear,
And the rocks melt with the sun;
I will luve thee still my dear,
When the sands of life shall run.
And fare thee weel, my only Luve,
And fare thee weel a while!
And I will come again, my Luve,
Tho' it were ten thousand mile.

ANNABEL LEE
—Edgar Allen Poe

It was many and many a year ago,
In a kingdom by the sea,
That a maiden there lived whom you may know
By the name of Annabel Lee;—
And this maiden she lived with no other thought
Than to love and be loved by me.
I was a child and she was a child,
In this kingdom by the sea;
But we loved with a love that was more than love—
I and my Annabel Lee—
With a love that the wingèd seraphs of Heaven
Coveted her and me.
And this was the reason that, long ago,
In this kingdom by the sea,
A wind blew out of a cloud, chilling
My beautiful Annabel Lee;
So that her high-born kinsmen came
And bore her away from me,
To shut her up in a sepulchre,
In this kingdom by the sea.
The angels, not half so happy in Heaven,
Went envying her and me—
Yes!—that was the reason (as all men know,
In this kingdom by the sea)
That the wind came out of the cloud by night,
Chilling and killing my Annabel Lee.
But our love it was stronger by far than the love
Of those who were older than we—
Of many far wiser than we—
And neither the angels in Heaven above,
Nor the demons down under the sea,
Can ever dissever my soul from the soul
Of the beautiful Annabel Lee.
For the moon never beams, without bringing me dreams
Of the beautiful Annabel Lee;

And the stars never rise, but I feel the bright eyes
Of the beautiful Annabel Lee:—
And so, all the night-tide, I lie down by the side
Of my darling—my darling—my life and my bride,
In her sepulchre there by the sea—
In her tomb by the sounding sea.

SWIFT THINGS ARE BEAUTIFUL
    —Elizabeth Coatsworth

Swift things are beautiful:
Swallow and deer,
And lightning that falls
Bright-veined and clear,
Rivers and meteors,
Wind in the wheat,
The strong-withered horse,
The runner's sure feet.

And slow things are beautiful:
The closing of day,
The pause of the wave
That curves downward to spray,
The ember that crumbles,
The opening flower,
And the ox that moves on
In the quiet of power.

THE CROCODILE
    —Lewis Carroll

How doth the little crocodile
    Improve his shining tail,
And pour the waters of the Nile
    On every golden scale!

How cheerfully he seems to grin!
    How neatly spread his claws,
And welcomes little fishes in
    With gently smiling jaws!

THE EAGLE
            —Alfred, Lord Tennyson

He clasps the crag with crooked hands;
Close to the sun in lonely lands,
Ring'd with the azure world, he stands.

The wrinkled sea beneath him crawls;
He watches from his mountain walls,
And like a thunderbolt he falls.

THE TIDE RISES, THE TIDE FALLS
       —Henry Wadsworth Longfellow

The tide rises, the tide falls,
The twilight darkens, the curlew calls;
Along the sea-sands damp and brown
The traveler hastens toward the town,
And the tide rises, the tide falls.
Darkness settles on roofs and walls,
But the sea, the sea in darkness calls;
The little waves, with their soft, white hands
Efface the footprints in the sands,
And the tide rises, the tide falls.
The morning breaks; the steeds in their stalls
Stamp and neigh, as the hostler calls;
The day returns, but nevermore
Returns the traveler to the shore.
And the tide rises, the tide falls.

MY HEART LEAPS UP WHEN I BEHOLD
   —William Wordsworth

MY heart leaps up when I behold
A rainbow in the sky:
So was it when my life began;
So is it now I am a man:
So be it when I shall grow old,
Or let me die!
The child is father of the man;
And I could wish my days to be
Bound each to each by natural piety.

YANKEE DOODLE
    —Anonymous

Yankee Doodle went to town
Riding on a pony,
Stuck a feather in his cap
And called it "macaroni."

Yankee Doodle, keep it up,
Yankee Doodle, dandy,
Mind the music and step,
And with the girls be handy.

Father and I went down to camp,
Along there we see the men and boys,
As thick as hasty pudding.

And there we see a thousand men,
As rich as 'Squire David;
And what they wasted every day,
I wish it could be saved,

The 'lasses they eat every day.
Would have so much that, I'll be bound,
They eat it when they're a mind to.

And there we see a swamping gun,
Large as a log of maple,
Upon a deuced little cart,
A load for father' cattle.

And every time they shot it off,
It takes a horn of powder,
And makes a noise like father's gun,
Only a nation louder.

THE FROG

        —Hilare Belloc

Be kind and tender to the Frog,
And do not call him names,
As "Slimy-skin, or "Polly-wog,"
Or likewise "Uncle James,"
Or "Gape-a-grin," or "Toad-gone-wrong,"
Or Billy Bandy-knees":
The frog is justly sensitive
To epithets like these.

No animal will more repay
A treatment kind and fair,
At least, so lonely people say
Who keep a frog (and by the way,
They are extremely rare).

MR. NOBODY
    —Anonymous

I know a funny little man,
As quiet as a mouse,
Who does the mischief that is done
In everybody's house!
There's no one ever sees his face,
And yet we all agree
That every plate we break was cracked
By Mr. Nobody.
'Tis he who always tears our books,
Who leaves the door ajar,
He pulls the buttons from our shirts,
And Scatters pins afar;
That squeaking door will always squeak,
For, Friend, don't you see,
We leave the oiling to be done
By Mr. Nobody.
He puts damp wood upon the fire,
That kettles cannot boil;
His are the feet that bring in the mud,
And all the carpets soil.
The papers always are mislaid,
Who had them last but he?
There's not one tosses them about
But Mr. Nobody.
The finger marks upon the door
By none of us are made;
We never leave the blinds unclosed,
to let the curtains fade;
The ink we never spill; the boots
That lying around you see
Are not our boots; they all belong
To Mr. Nobody!

THE BELLS
   —Edgar Allen Poe

HEAR the sledges with the bells--
Silver bells--
What a world of merriment their melody foretells!
How they tinkle, tinkle, tinkle,
In the icy air of night!
While the stars that oversprinkle
All the heavens, seem to twinkle
With a crystalline delight;
Keeping time, time, time,
In a sort of Runic rhyme,
To the tintinnabulation that so musically wells
From the bells, bells, bells, bells,
Bells, bells, bells,--
From the jingling and the tinkling of the bells.
Hear the mellow wedding-bells,
Golden bells!
What a world of happiness their harmony foretells!
Through the balmy air of night
How they ring out their delight
From the molten-golden notes!
And all in tune,
What a liquid ditty floats
To the turtle-dove that listens, while she gloats
On the moon!
Oh, from out the sounding cells,
What a gust of euphony voluminously wells!
How it swells!
How it dwells
On the Future!
how it tells
Of rapture that impels
To the swinging and the ringing
Of the bells, bells, bells--
Of the bells, bells, bells, bells,
Bells, bells, bells--

To the rhyming and the chiming of the bells!
Hear the loud alarum bells--
Brazen bells!
What a tale of terror, now, their turbulency tells!
In the startled ear of night
How they scream out their affright!
Too much horrified to speak,
They can only shriek, shriek,
Out of tune,
In a clamorous appealing to the mercy of the fire,
In a mad expostulation with the deaf and frantic fire
Leaping higher, higher, higher
With a desperate desire,
And a resolute endeavor,
Now--now to sit or never,
By the side of the pale-faced moon.
Oh, the bells, bells, bells!
What a tale their terror tells
Of despair!
How they clang, and clash, and roar!
What a horror they out pour
On the bosom of the palpitating air!
Yet the ear, it fully knows,
By the twanging
And the clanging,
How the danger ebbs and flows;
Yet the ear distinctly tells,
In the jangling
And the wrangling,
How the danger sinks and swells,
By the sinking of the swelling in the anger of the bells--
Of the bells--
Of the bells, bells, bells, bells,
Bells, bells, bells,--
In the clamor and the clangor of the bells!
Hear the tolling of the bells--
Iron bells!
What a world of solemn thought their monody compels!
In a silence of the night

How we shiver with affright
At the melancholy menace of their tone!
For every sound that floats
From the rust within their throats,
Is a groan:
And the people--ah, the people--
They that dwell up in the steeple,
All alone, And who, tolling, tolling, tolling,
In that muffled monotone,
Feel a glory in so rolling
On the human heart a stone--
They are neither man nor woman--
They are neither brute nor human--
They are Ghouls!
And their king it is who tolls;
And he rolls, rolls, rolls, rolls,
A paean from the bells!
And his merry bosom swells
With the paean of the bells!
And he dances and he yells;
Keeping time, time, time
In a sort of Runic rhyme,
To the paean of the bells--
Of the bells;
Keeping time, time, time,
In a sort of Runic rhyme,
To the throbbing of the bells--
Of the bells, bells, bells,
To the sobbing of the bells;
Keeping time, time, time,
As he knells, knells, knells,
In a happy Runic rhyme,
To the rolling of the bells,--
Of the bells, bells, bells--
To the tolling of the bells,
Of the bells, bells, bells, bells,
Bells, bells, bells,--
To the moaning and the groaning of the bells.

WOODMAN, SPARE THAT TREE!
  —George Pope Morris

Woodman, Spare That Tree!
Touch not a single bough!
In youth it sheltered me,
And I'll protect it now.

"Twas my forefather' hand
That placed it near his cot;
There, woodman, let it stand,
Thy ax shall harm it not!

That old familiar tree,
Whose glory and renown
Are spread o'er land and sea,
And wouldst thou hew it down?

Woodman, forbear thy stroke!
Cut not its earth-bound ties!
Oh! spare that aged oak;
Now towering to the skies.

When but an idle boy
I sought its grateful joy
In all their gushing joy
Here too my sisters played.

My mother kissed me here
My father pressed my hand—
Forgive this foolish tear,
But let that old oak stand!

My heart-strings round thee cling,
Close as thy bark, old friend!
Here shall thy branches bend.
And still thy branches bend.

Old tree, the storm still brave!
And, woodman, leave the spot!
While I've a hand to save,
Thy ax shall harm it not.

DO YOU CARROT ALL FOR ME?
    —Anonymous

Do you carrot all for me?
My heart beets for you,
With your turnip nose
And your radish face,
You are a peach.
If we cantaloupe,
Lettuce marry;
Weed make a swell pear.

THE WALRUS AND THE CARPENTER
—Lewis Carroll

The sun was shining on the sea,
Shining with all his might:
He did his very best to make
The billows smooth and bright--
And this was odd, because it was
The middle of the night.
The moon was shining sulkily,
Because she thought the sun
Had got no business to be there
After the day was done--
"It's very rude of him," she said,
"To come and spoil the fun!"
The sea was wet as wet could be,
The sands were dry as dry.
You could not see a cloud, because
No cloud was in the sky:
No birds were flying overhead--
There were no birds to fly.
The Walrus and the Carpenter
Were walking close at hand;
They wept like anything to see
Such quantities of sand:
"If this were only cleared away,"
They said, "it would be grand!"
"If seven maids with seven mops
Swept it for half a year.
Do you suppose," the Walrus said,
"That they could get it clear?"
"I doubt it," said the Carpenter,
And shed a bitter tear.
"O Oysters, come and walk with us!"
The Walrus did beseech.
"A pleasant walk, a pleasant talk,
Along the briny beach:
We cannot do with more than four,
To give a hand to each."

The eldest Oyster looked at him,
But never a word he said:
The eldest Oyster winked his eye,
And shook his heavy head--
Meaning to say he did not choose
To leave the oyster-bed.
But four young Oysters hurried up,
All eager for the treat:
Their coats were brushed, their faces washed,
Their shoes were clean and neat--
And this was odd, because, you know,
They hadn't any feet.
Four other Oysters followed them,
And yet another four;
And thick and fast they came at last,
And more, and more, and more--
All hopping through the frothy waves,
And scrambling to the shore.
 The Walrus and the Carpenter
Walked on a mile or so,
And then they rested on a rock
Conveniently low:
And all the little Oysters stood
And waited in a row.
"The time has come," the Walrus said,
"To talk of many things:
Of shoes--and ships--and sealing-wax--
Of cabbages--and kings--
And why the sea is boiling hot--
And whether pigs have wings."
"But wait a bit," the Oysters cried,
"Before we have our chat;
For some of us are out of breath,
And all of us are fat!"
"No hurry!" said the Carpenter.
They thanked him much for that.
"A loaf of bread," the Walrus said,
"Is what we chiefly need:

We can begin to feed."
"But not on us!" the Oysters cried,
We can begin to feed."
"But not on us!" the Oysters cried,
Turning a little blue.
"After such kindness, that would be
A dismal thing to do!"
"The night is fine," the Walrus said.
"Do you admire the view?
"It was so kind of you to come!
And you are very nice!"
The Carpenter said nothing but
"Cut us another slice:
I wish you were not quite so deaf--
I've had to ask you twice!"
"It seems a shame," the Walrus said,
"To play them such a trick,
After we've brought them out so far,
And made them trot so quick!"
The Carpenter said nothing but
"The butter's spread too thick!"
"I weep for you," the Walrus said:
"I deeply sympathize."
With sobs and tears he sorted out
Those of the largest size,
Holding his pocket-handkerchief
Before his streaming eyes.
"O Oysters," said the Carpenter,
"You've had a pleasant run!
Shall we be trotting home again?'
But answer came there none--
And this was scarcely odd, because
They'd eaten every one.

LOVE AND FRIENDSHIP
   —Emily Brontë

Love is like the wild rose-briar,
Friendship like the holly-tree—
The holly is dark when the rose-briar blooms
But which will bloom most constantly?
The wild-rose briar is sweet in the spring,
Its summer blossoms scent the air;
Yet wait till winter comes again
And who will call the wild-briar fair?
Then scorn the silly rose-wreath now
And deck thee with the holly's sheen,
That, when December blights thy brow,
He may still leave thy garland green.

BILLY BOY
       —Anonymous

Oh, where have you been, Billy boy, Billy boy,
Oh, where have you been, charming Billy?
I have been to seek a wife, she's the joy of my young life,
She's a young thing and cannot leave her mother.

Did she ask you to come in, Billy boy, Billy boy,
Did she ask you to come in charming Billy?
She did ask me to come in, with a dimple in her chin,
She's a young thing and cannot leave her mother.

Did she ask you to sit down, Billy boy, Billy boy,
Did she ask you to sit down charming Billy?
She did ask me to sit down with a curtsey to the ground,
She a young thing and cannot leave her mother.

Did she set for you a chair, Billy boy, Billy boy,
Did she set you a chair, charming Billy?
Yes, she set for me a chair, she got ringlets in her hair,
She a young thing and cannot leave her mother.

How old is she, Billy boy, Billy boy
How old is she charming Billy?
She's three times six, four times seven,
twenty-eight, and eleven.
She a young thing and cannot leave her mother.

How tall is she, Billy boy, Billy boy
How tall is she charming Billy?
She's as tall as any pine and as straight as a pumpkin vine,
She a young thing and cannot leave her mother.

Can she bake a cherry pie, Billy boy, Billy boy
Can she make a cherry pie, charming Billy?
She can make a cherry pie, quick as a cat can wink her eye.
She a young thing and cannot leave her mother.

74

Does she often go to church, Billy boy, Billy boy,
Does she often go to church, charming Billy?
Yes, she often goes to church, with her bonnet white as birch,
She a young thing and cannot leave her mother.

Can she make a pudding well, Billy boy, Billy boy
Can she make a pudding well, harming Billy?
She can make a pudding well, I can tell it by the smell,
She a young thing and cannot leave her mother.

Can she make a feather-bed, Billy boy, Billy boy,
Can she make a feather-bed charming Billy?
She can make a feather-bed, place the pillows at the head,
She a young thing and cannot leave her mother.

Can she card and can she spin, Billy boy, Billy boy,
Can she card and can she spin, charming Billy?
She can card and she can spin, she can do most anything,
She a young thing and cannot leave her mother.

A LITTLE LEARNING
      —Alexander Pope

A little learning is a dangerous thing;
Drink deep, or taste not the Pierian spring:
There shallow draughts intoxicate the brain,
And drinking largely sobers us again.
Fired at first sight with what the Muse imparts,
In fearless youth we tempt the heights of Arts;
While from the bounded level of our mind
Short views we take, nor see the lengths behind,
But, more advanced, behold with strange surprise
New distant scenes of endless science rise!
So pleased at first the towering Alps we try,
Mount o'er the vales, and seem to tread the sky;
The eternal snows appear already past,
And the first clouds and mountains seem the last;
But those attained, we tremble to survey
The growing labours of the lengthened way;
The increasing prospect tires our wandering eyes,
Hill peep o'er hills, and Alps on Alps arise!

THE SEA AND THE SKYLARK
    —Gerard Manley Hopkins

On ear and ear noises too old to end
Trench right, the tide that ramps against the shore;
With a flood or a fall, low lull-off or all roar,
Frequenting there while moon shall wear and wend.
Left hand, off land, I hear the lark ascend,
His rash-fresh re-winded new-skeinèd score
In crisps of curl off wild winch whirl, and pour
And pelt music, till none's to spill nor spend.
How these two shame this shallow and frail town!
How ring right out our sordid turbid time,
Being pure ! We, life's pride and cared-for crown,
Have lost that cheer and charm of earth's past prime:
Our make and making break, are breaking, down
To man's last dust, drain fast towards man's first slime.

I REMEMBER, I REMEMBER
   —Thomas Hood

I remember, I remember,
The house where I was born,
The little window where the sun
Came peeping in at morn;
He never came a wink too soon,
Nor brought too long a day,
But now, I often wish the night
Had borne my breath away!
I remember, I remember,
The roses, red and white,
The violets, and the lily-cups,
Those flowers made of light!
The lilacs where the robin built,
And where my brother set
The laburnum on his birthday, -
The tree is living yet!

I remember, I remember,
Where I was used to swing,
And thought the air must rush as fresh
To swallows on the wing;
My spirit flew in feathers then,
That is so heavy now,
And summer pools could hardly cool
The fever on my brow!
I remember, I remember,
The fir trees dark and high;
I used to think their slender tops
Were close against the sky:
It was a childish ignorance,
But now 'tis little joy
To know I'm farther off from heaven

UPHILL

—Christina Rossetti

Does the road wind uphill all the way?
Yes, to the very end.
Will the day's journey take the whole long day?
From morn to night, my friend.
But is there for the night a resting-place?
A roof for when the slow, dark hours begin.
May not the darkness hide it from my face?
You cannot miss that inn.
Shall I meet other wayfarers at night?
Those who have gone before.
Then must I knock, or call when just in sight?
They will not keep you standing at that door.
Shall I find comfort, travel-sore and weak?
Of labour you shall find the sum.
Will there be beds for me and all who seek?
Yea, beds for all who come.

AS KINGFISHERS CATCH FIRE
        —Gerard Manley Hopkins

As kingfishers catch fire, dragonflies, draw flame;
As tumbled over rim in roundy wells
Stones ring; like each tucked string tells, each hung bell's
Bow swung finds tongue to fling out broad its name;
Each mortal thing does one thing and the same:
Deals out that being indoors each one dwells;
Selves— goes itself; myself it speaks and spells,
Crying what I do is me: for that I came.
I say more: the just man justices;
Keeps grace: that keeps all his goings graces;
Acts in God's eye what in God's eye he is—
Christ— for Christ plays in ten thousand places,
Lovely in limbs, and lovely in eyes not his
To the Father through the features of men's faces.

ARIEL'S SONGS
        —William Shakespeare
(i)
Come unto these yellow sands,
And then take hands:
Curtsied when you have, and kissed
The wild waves whist,
Foot it featly here and there;
And, sweet sprites, the burden bear.
Hark, hark!
Bow, wow
The watch-dogs bark,
Bow, wow,
Hark, hark! I hear
The strain of strutting Chanticleer
Cry, Cock-a-diddle-dow.
(ii)
Full fathom five thy father lies;
Of his bones are coral made;
Those are pearls that were his eyes:
Nothing of him that doth fade,
But doth suffer a sea-change
Into something rich and strange:
Sea nymphs hourly ring his knell.
Ding-dong!
Hark! now I hear them,
Ding-dong, bell!
(iii)
Where the bee sucks, there suck I,
In a cowslip's bell I lie,
There I couch when owls do cry,
On the bat's back I do fly
After summer merrily.
Merrily, merrily, shall I live now
Under the blossom that hangs on the bough.

SONNET 8
    —William Shakespeare

Music to hear, why hear'st thou music sadly?
Sweets with sweets war not, joy delights in joy.
Why lov'st thou that which thou receiv'st not gladly,
Or else receiv'st with pleasure thine annoy?
If the true concord of well-tunèd sounds
By unions married do offend thine ear,
They do but sweetly chide thee, who confounds
In singleness the parts that thou shouldst bear.
Mark how one string, sweet husband to another,
Strikes each in each by mutual ordering,
Resembling sire and child and happy mother,
Who all in one one pleasing note do sing;
Whose speechless song, being many, seeming one,
Sings this to thee: 'Thou single wilt prove none.'

THE PASSIONATE SHEPHERD TO HIS LOVE
—Christopher Marlowe

Come live with me and be my love,
And we will all the pleasures prove,
That hills and valleys, dales and fields,
And all the craggy mountains yields.
There we will sit upon the rocks,
And see the shepherds feed their flocks,
By shallow rivers to whose falls
Melodious birds sing madrigals.
And I will make thee beds of roses
With a thousand fragrant posies,
A cap of flowers, and a kirtle
Embroidered all with leaves of myrtle;
A gown made of the finest wool
Which from our pretty lambs we pull;
Fair linèd slippers for the cold,
With buckles of the purest gold;
A belt of straw and ivy buds,
With coral clasps and amber studs:
And if these pleasures may thee move,
Come live with me and be my love.
The shepherds' swains shall dance and sing
For thy delight each May morning:
If these delights thy mind may move,
Then live with me and be my love.

ON HIS BLINDNESS
—John Milton

When I consider how my light is spent,
Ere half my days, in this dark world and wide,
And that one talent which is death to hide
Lodged with me useless, though my soul more bent
To serve therewith my Maker, and present
My true account, lest he returning chide,
'Doth God exact day-labour, light denied?
I fondly ask. But Patience, to prevent
That murmur, soon replies: 'God doth not need
Either man's work or his own gifts; who best
Bear his mild yoke, they serve him best. His state
Is kingly: thousands at his bidding speed,
And post o'er land and ocean without rest;
They also serve who only stand and await.

HAMLET, ACT 3, SCENE 1
   —William Shakespeare

To be, or not to be: that is the question:
Whether 'tis nobler in the mind to suffer
The slings and arrows of outrageous fortune,
Or to take arms against a sea of troubles,
And by opposing end them? To die: to sleep;
No more; and by a sleep to say we end
The heart-ache and the thousand natural shocks
That flesh is heir to, 'tis a consummation
Devoutly to be wish'd. To die, to sleep;
To sleep: perchance to dream: ay, there's the rub;
For in that sleep of death what dreams may come
When we have shuffled off this mortal coil,
Must give us pause: there's the respect
That makes calamity of so long life;
For who would bear the whips and scorns of time,
The oppressor's wrong, the proud man's contumely,
The pangs of despised love, the law's delay,
The insolence of office and the spurns
That patient merit of the unworthy takes,
When he himself might his quietus make
With a bare bodkin? who would fardels bear,
To grunt and sweat under a weary life,
But that the dread of something after death,
The undiscover'd country from whose bourn
No traveller returns, puzzles the will
And makes us rather bear those ills we have
Than fly to others that we know not of?
Thus conscience does make cowards of us all;
And thus the native hue of resolution
Is sicklied o'er with the pale cast of thought,
And enterprises of great pith and moment
With this regard their currents turn awry,
And lose the name of action.--Soft you now!
The fair Ophelia! Nymph, in thy orisons
Be all my sins remember'd.

THE WAY THROUGH THE WOODS
    —Rudyard Kipling

They shut the road through the woods
Seventy years ago.
Weather and rain have undone it again,
And now you would never know
There was once a road through the woods
Before they planted the trees.
It is underneath the coppice and heath
And the thin anemones.
Only the keeper sees
That, where the ring-dove broods,
And the badgers roll at ease,
There was once a road through the woods.
Yet, if you enter the woods
Of a summer evening late,
When the night-air cools on the trout-ringed pools
Where the otter whistles his mate,
(They fear not men in the woods,
Because the see so few)
You will hear the beat of a horse's feet,
And the swish of a skirt in the dew,
Steadily cantering through
The misty solitudes,
As though they perfectly knew
The old lost road through the woods. . . .
But there is no road through the woods.

IF

—Rudyard Kipling

If you can keep your head when all about you
  Are losing theirs and blaming it on you,
If you can trust yourself when all men doubt you,
  But make allowance for their doubting too;
If you can wait and not be tired of waiting,
  Or being lied about, don't deal in lies,
Or being hated don't give way to hating
  And yet don't look too good, nor talk too wise:
If you can dream—and not make dreams your master;
  If you can think—and not make thoughts your aim,
If you can meet with Triumph and Disaster
  And treat those two imposters just the same;
If you can bear to hear the truth you've spoken
  Twisted by knaves to make a trap for fools,
Or watch the things you gave your life to, broken,
  And stoop and build 'em up with worn-out tools;

If you can make one heap of all your winnings
  And risk it on one turn of pitch-and-toss,
And lose, and start again at your beginnings
  And never breathe a word about your loss;
If you can force your heart and nerve and sinew
  To serve your turn long after they are gone,
And so hold on when there is nothing in you
  Except the Will which says to them: "Hold on!"

If you can talk with crowds and keep your virtue,
  Or walk with Kings—nor lose the common touch,
If neither foes nor loving friends can hurt you,
  If all men count with you, none too much;
If you can fill the unforgiving minute
  With sixty seconds' worth of distance run,
Yours is the Earth and everything that's in it,
  And—which is more—you'll be a Man, my son!

TO CELIA
—Ben Jonson

Drink to me only with thine eyes,
And I will pledge with mine ;
Or leave a kiss but in the cup
And I'll not look for wine.
The thirst that from the soul doth rise
Doth ask a drink divine ;
But might I of Jove's nectar sup,
I would not change for thine.
I sent thee late a rosy wreath,
Not so much honouring thee
As giving it a hope that there
It could not withered be ;
But thou thereon didst only breathe,
And sent'st it back to me ;
Since when it grows, and smells, I swear,
Not of itself but thee !

ODE TO A NIGHTINGALE
    —John Keats

I
My heart aches, and a drowsy numbness pains
My sense, as though of hemlock I had drunk,
Or emptied some dull opiate to the drains
One minute past, and Lethe-wards had sunk :
'Tis not through envy of thy happy lot,
But being too happy in thy happiness, -
That thou, light-wingèd Dryad of the trees,
In some melodious plot
Of beechen green, and shadows numberless,
Singest of summer in full-throated ease.

2
O for a draught of vintage ! that hath been
Cool'd a long age in the deep-delvèd earth,
Tasting of Flora and the country-green,
Dance, and Provençal song, and sunburnt mirth !
O for a beaker full of the warm South !
Full of the true, the blushful Hippocrene,
With beaded bubbles winking at the brim,
And purple-stainèd mouth ;
That I might drink, and leave the world unseen,
And with thee fade away into the forest dim :

3
Fade far away, dissolve, and quite forget
What thou among the leaves hast never known,
The weariness, the fever, and the fret
Here, where men sit and hear each other groan ;
Where palsy shakes a few, sad, last grey hairs,
Where youth grows pale, and spectre-thin, and dies ;
Where but to think is to be full of sorrow
And leaden-eyed despairs ;
Where Beauty cannot keep her lustrous eyes,
Or new Love pine at them beyond tomorrow.

4
Away ! away! for I will fly to thee,
Not charioted by Bacchus and his pards,

Though the dull brain perplexes and retards :
Already with thee ! tender is the night,
And haply the Queen-Moon is on her throne,
Cluster'd around by all her starry Fays ;
But here there is no light,
Save what from heaven is with the breezes blown,
Through verdurous glooms and winding mossy ways.

5
I cannot see what flowers are at my feet,
Nor what soft incense hangs upon the boughs,
But, in embalmèd darkness, guess each sweet
Wherewith the seasonable month endows
The grass, the thicket, and the fruit-tree wild ;
White hawthorn, and the pastoral eglantine ;
Fast fading violets cover'd up in leaves ;
And mid-May's eldest child,
The coming musk-rose, full of dewy wine,
The murmurous haunt of flies on summer eves.
6
Darkling I listen ; and for many a time
I have been half in love with easeful Death,
Call'd him soft names in many a musèd rhyme,
To take into the air my quiet breath ;
Now more than ever seems it rich to die,
To cease upon the midnight with no pain,
While thou art pouring forth thy soul abroad
In such an ecstasy !
Still wouldst thou sing, and I have ears in vain -
To thy high requiem become a sod.
7
Thou wast not born for death, immortal Bird !
No hungry generations tread thee down ;
The voice I hear this passing night was heard
In ancient days by emperor and clown :
Perhaps the self-same song that found a path
Through the sad heart of Ruth, when, sick for home,
She stood in tears amid the alien corn ;

The same that oft-times hath
Charm'd magic casements, opening on the foam
Of perilous seas, in faery lands forlorn.
8
Forlorn ! the very word is like a bell
To toll me back from thee to my sole self !
Adieu ! the fancy cannot cheat so well
As she is fam'd to do, deceiving elf.
Adieu ! adieu ! thy plaintive anthem fades
Past the near meadows, over the still stream,
Up the hill-side ; and now 'tis buried deep
In the next valley-glades :
Was it a vision, or a waking dream?

SWEET AND LOW
        —Alfred, Lord Tennyson

Sweet and low, sweet and low,
Wind of the western sea,
Low, low, breathe and blow,
Wind of the western sea!
Over the rolling waters go,
Come from the dying moon, and blow,
Blow him again to me;
While my little one, while my pretty one, sleeps.

Sleep and rest, sleep and rest,
Father will come to thee soon;
Rest, rest on mother's breast,
Father will come to thee soon;
Father will come to his babe in the nest,
Sliver sails all out of the west
Under the silver moon;
Sleep, .my little one, sleep, my pretty one, sleep.

SONNET 14
—William Shakespeare

Not from the stars do I my judgement pluck,
And yet me thinks I have astronomy ;
But not to tell of good or evil luck,
Of plagues, of dearths, or seasons' quality.
Nor can I fortune to brief minutes tell,
'Pointing to each his thunder, rain, and wind,
Or say with princes if it shall go well
By oft predict that I in heaven find ;
But from thine eyes my knowledge I derive,
And, constant stars, in them I read such art
As truth and beauty shall together thrive
If from thyself to store thou wouldst convert.
Or else of thee this I prognosticate :
Thy end is truth's and beauty's doom and date.

KUBLA KHAN
   —Samuel Taylor Coleridge

In Xanadu did Kubla Khan
A stately pleasure-dome decree :
Where Alph, the sacred river, ran
Through caverns measureless to man
Down to a sunless sea.
So twice five miles of fertile ground
With walls and towers were girdled round :
And there were gardens bright with sinuous rills
Where blossomed many an incense-bearing tree;
And here were forests ancient as the hills,
Enfolding sunny spots of greenery.
But O, that deep romantic chasm which slanted
Down the green hill athwart a cedarn cover!
A savage place! as holy and enchanted
As e'er beneath a waning moon was haunted
By woman wailing for her demon-lover!
And from this chasm, with ceaseless turmoil seething,
As if this earth in fast thick pants were breathing,
A mighty fountain momently was forced;
Amid whose swift half-intermitted burst
Huge fragments vaulted like rebounding hail,
Or chaffy grain beneath the thresher's flail :
And 'mid these dancing rocks at once and ever
It flung up momently the sacred river.
Five miles meandering with a mazy motion
Through wood and dale the sacred river ran,
Then reached the caverns measureless to man,
And sank in tumult to a lifeless ocean :
And 'mid this tumult Kubla heard from far
Ancestral voices prophesying war!
The shadow of the dome of pleasure
Floated midway on the waves;
Where was heard the mingled measure
Where was heard the mingled measure
From the fountain and the caves.

It was a miracle or rare devices,
A sunny pleasure-dome with caves of ice!
A damsel with a dulcimer
In a vision once I saw :
It was an Abyssinian maid,
And on her dulcimer she played,
Singing of Mount Abora.
Could I revive within me,
Her symphony and song,
To such a deep delight 'twould win me,
That with music loud and long,
I would build that dome in air,
That sunny dome! those caves of ice!
And all who heard should see them there,
And all should cry, Beware! Beware!
His flashing eyes, his floating hair!
Weave a circle round him thrice,
And close your eyes with holy dread,
For he on honey-dew hath fed,
And drunk the milk of Paradise.

THE KISS
   —Sara Teasdale

I HOPED that he would love me,
And he has kissed my mouth, But I am like a stricken bird
That cannot reach the south.

For though I know he loves me,
 To-night my heart is sad; His kiss was not so wonderful
As all the dreams I had.

COME
    —Sara Teasdale

COME, when the pale moon like a petal
Floats in the pearly dusk of spring,
Come with outstretched arms to take me,
Come with lips pursed up to cling.

Come, for life is a frail moth flying
Caught in the web of the years that pass,
And soon we two, so warm and eager,
Will be as the gray stones in the grass.

WHAT IS LOVE?
        —Ernest Dowson

  What is Love?
Is it a folly,
Is it mirth, or melancholy?
  Joys above,
Are there many, or not any?
  What is Love?

  If you please,
A most sweet folly!
Full of mirth and melancholy:
  Both of these!
In its sadness worth all gladness,
  If you please!

  Prithee where,
Goes Love a-hiding?
Is he long in his abiding
  Anywhere?
Can you bind him when you find him;
  Prithee, where?

  With spring days
Love comes and dallies:
Upon the mountains, through the valleys
  Lie Love's ways.
Then he leaves you and deceives you
  In spring days.

ON THE GRASSHOPPER AND CRICKET
        —JOHN KEATS

The poetry of earth is never dead:
  When all the birds are faint with the hot sun,
  And hide in cooling trees, a voice will run
From hedge to hedge about the new-mown mead;
That is the Grasshopper's—he takes the lead
  In summer luxury,—he has never done
  With his delights; for when tired out with fun
He rests at ease beneath some pleasant weed.
The poetry of earth is ceasing never:
  On a lone winter evening, when the frost
    Has wrought a silence, from the stove there shrills
The Cricket's song, in warmth increasing ever,
  And seems to one in drowsiness half lost,
    The Grasshopper's among some grassy hills.

BRIGHT STAR! WOULD I WERE STEADFAST AS THOU ART
      —John Keats

Bright star! would I were steadfast as thou art—
   Not in lone splendor hung aloft the night,
And watching, with eternal lids apart,
   Like Nature's patient sleepless Eremite,
The moving waters at their priest like task
   Of pure ablution round earth's human shores,
Or gazing on the new soft fallen mask
   Of snow upon the mountains and the moors—
No—yet still steadfast, still unchangeable,
   Pillow'd upon my fair love's ripening breast,
To feel for ever its soft fall and swell,
   Awake for ever in a sweet unrest,
Still, still to hear her tender-taken breath,
And so live ever—or else swoon to death.

'TIS MOONLIGHT
—Emily Brontë

'TIS moonlight, summer moonlight,
All soft and still and fair;
The solemn hour of midnight
Breathes sweet thoughts everywhere,

But most where trees are sending
Their breezy boughs on high,
Or stooping low are lending
A shelter from the sky.

And there in those wild bowers
A lovely form is laid;
Green grass and dew-steeped flowers
Wave gently round her head.

CHARGE OF THE LIGHT BRIGADE
     —Alfred Lord Tennyson

Half a league, half a league,
Half a league onward,
All in the valley of Death
Rode the six hundred. "Forward, the Light Brigade!
Charge for the guns!" he said:
Into the valley of Death
Rode the six hundred.

"Forward, the Light Brigade!"
Was there a man dismayed?
Not tho' the soldiers knew
Someone had blundered: Theirs was not to make reply,
Theirs was not to reason why,
Theirs was but to do and die:
Into the valley of Death
Rode the six hundred.

Cannon to the right of them,
Cannon to the left of them,
Cannon in front of them
Volleyed and thunder'd; Storm'd at with shot and shell,
Boldly they rode and well,
Into the jaws of Death,
Into the mouth of Hell,
Rode the six hundred.

Flashed all their sabres bare,
Flashed as they turned in air,
Sab'ring the gunners there,
Charging an army, while
All the world wondered:
Plunging in the battery smoke,
Right through the line they broke; Cossack and Russian
Reeled from the sabre-stroke
Shattered and sundered. Then they rode back, but not--
Not the six hundred.

Cannon to the right of them,
Cannon to the left of them,
Cannon in front of them
Volleyed and thundered; Stormed at with shot and shell,
 While horse and hero fell,
They that fought so well,
Came thro' the jaws of Death,
Back from the mouth of Hell,
All that was left of them,
Left of the six hundred.

When can their glory fade?
Oh, the wild charge they made!
All the world wondered. Honor the charge they made!
Honor the Light Brigade,
Noble Six Hundred!

AMERICA THE BEAUTIFUL
—Katharine Lee Bates

O BEAUTIFUL for spacious skies,
For amber waves of grain, For purple mountain majesties
 Above the fruited plain! America! America!
God shed his grace on thee And crown thy good with brotherhood
From sea to shining sea!

O beautiful for pilgrim feet,
 Whose stern, impassioned stress A thoroughfare for freedom beat
 Across the wilderness! America! America!
God mend thy every flaw, Confirm thy soul in self-control,
Thy liberty in law!

O beautiful for heroes proved
In liberating strife, Who more than self their country loved,
 And mercy more than life! America! America!
May God thy gold refine, Till all success be nobleness
 And every gain divine!

O beautiful for patriot dream
That sees beyond the years Thine alabaster cities gleam
Undimmed by human tears! America! America!
God shed his grace on thee And crown thy good with brotherhood
From sea to shining sea!

BEAUTIFUL SOUP
     —Lewis Carroll

BEAUTIFUL Soup, so rich and green,
Waiting in a hot tureen!
Who for such dainties would not stoop?
Soup of the evening, beautiful Soup!
Soup of the evening, beautiful Soup!

Beau--ootiful Soo-oop! Beau--ootiful Soo-oop!
Soo--oop of the e--e--evening,
Beautiful, beautiful Soup!

Beautiful Soup! Who cares for fish,
Game, or any other dish?
Who would not give all else for two
Pennyworth only of Beautiful Soup?
Pennyworth only of beautiful Soup?

Beau--ootiful Soo-oop! Beau--ootiful Soo-oop!
Soo--oop of the e--e--evening,
Beautiful, beauti--FUL SOUP!

WHEN I HAVE FEARS THAT I MAY CEASE TO BE
    —John Keats

When I have fears that I may cease to be
    Before my pen has glean'd my teeming brain,
Before high piled books, in charact'ry,
    Hold like rich garners the full-ripen'd grain;
When I behold, upon the night's starr'd face,
    Huge cloudy symbols of a high romance,
And think that I may never live to trace
    Their shadows, with the magic hand of chance;
And when I feel, fair creature of an hour!
    That I shall never look upon thee more,
Never have relish in the faery power
    Of unreflecting love!—then on the shore
Of the wide world I stand alone, and think
Till Love and Fame to nothingness do sink.

THE VOICE OF THE LOBSTER
    —Lewis Carroll

"'TIS the voice of the Lobster: I heard him declare
'You have baked me too brown, I must sugar my hair.'
As a duck with its eyelids, so he with his nose
Trims his belt and his buttons, and turns out his toes.
When the sands are all dry, he is gay as a lark,
And will talk in contemptuous tones of the Shark:
But, when the tide rises and sharks are around,
His voice has a timid and tremulous sound."

"I passed by his garden, and marked, with one eye,
How the Owl and the Panther were sharing a pie:
The Panther took pie-crust, and gravy, and meat,
While the Old had the dish as its share of the treat.
When the pie was all finished, the Owl, as a boon,
Was kindly permitted to pocket the spoon:
While the Panther received knife and fork with a growl,
And concluded the banquet by [eating the owl.]

THE BEST THING IN THE WORLD
        —Elizabeth Barrett Browning

WHAT'S the best thing in the world?
June-rose, by May-dew impearled;
Sweet south-wind, that means no rain;
 Truth, not cruel to a friend;
Pleasure, not in haste to end;
 Beauty, not self-decked and curled
Till its pride is over-plain;
 Love, when, so, you're loved again.
What's the best thing in the world?
--Something out of it, I think.

MY SOUL IS AWAKENED
       —Anne Brontë

MY soul is awakened, my spirit is soaring,
  And carried aloft on the wings of the breeze;
For, above, and around me, the wild wind is roaring,
  Arousing to rapture the earth and the seas.

The long withered grass in the sunshine is glancing,
  The bare trees are tossing their branches on high;
The dead leaves beneath them are merrily dancing,
  The white clouds are scudding across the blue sky.

I wish I could see how the ocean is lashing
The foam of its billows to whirlwinds of spray,
I wish I could see how its proud waves are dashing
And hear the wild roar of their thunder today!

ON THE WEDDING OF THE AERONAUT
    —Ambrose Bierce

AERONAUT, you're fairly caught,
Despite your bubble's leaven: Out of the skies a lady's eyes
Have brought you down to Heaven!

 No more, no more you'll freely soar
 Above the grass and gravel:
Henceforth you'll walk--and she will chalk
The line that you're to travel!

TO MY DEAR AND LOVING HUSBAND
      —Anne Bradstreet

IF ever two were one then surely we.
If ever man were loved by wife, then thee;
If ever wife were happy in a man,
Compare with me, ye women, if you can.
I prize thy love more than whole mines of gold
Or all the riches that the East doth hold.
My love is such that rivers cannot quench,
Nor aught but love from thee give recompense.
Thy love is such I can no way repay,
The heavens reward thee manifold, I pray.
Then while we live, in love let's so perservere
That when we live no more, we may live ever.

Peter Beeson Interview

Peter Beeson was born in 1945 in San Antonio, Texas. He holds PhD in Medical Sociology from the University of Nebraska-Lincoln. He is married and has one daughter, Mary Elizabeth. Peter spent most of his career working for the State of Nebraska in health and human services; primarily in mental health. He has also held several academic appointments and has to his credit a number of academic and work-related publications. He is past President of the National Association for Rural Mental and recipient of the Victory I. Howery Award for significant contributions to rural mental health. He is also a photographer and author with essays and photo essays published in local as well as national magazines. He is currently "retired" and spends his time writing and doing photography.

Glazner: You are writing about your experience with Alzheimer's in your poetry and in a memoir, could you talk about what you hope to accomplish by documenting your experience in writing?

Beeson: I don't know if I have any mission or goals. I think, in part, it is a way for me to come to grips with what's going on with me and use the writing as a vehicle to work through things. I think it is also a way in which I can leave something for people I am close with, to leave an accounting for my wife and daughter. Once things get worse or I disappear or whatever, through the poetry they might have a little bit more of an understanding of what it's been like for me and, if my daughter ever has children, it will be a way for them to get a picture of me and what happened to me. And, I suppose I'd like to think that it may give others (victims, family members, policy makers, the public, etc.) a little perspective on the illness and provide a broader context in which to look at people with this illness.

Glazner: Have you read your family the poems you have written?

Beeson: No, I have showed them some of the poems, but not of all them. It seemed to make them sad and so I've stopped.

Glazner: How old is your daughter?

Beeson: She's eighteen years old and just graduated from high school. Next year she heads off to Purdue University to major in Chemical Engineering. And, while it will be sad for me to have her so far away, I'm glad that she won't be close and have to experience daily my deterioration and mental decline.

Glazner: I read your poems to the poetry class I teach at Desert Academy, in Santa Fe and the students found your poems to be powerful, disturbing and sad.

Beeson: (Laughs) It is sad!

Glazner: Yes, no doubt about it, but you also write with some humor and a certain toughness. It seems like it is in your nature to write, given your long history of publications.

Beeson: Yes, I suppose so. It seems like I've always written and I do keep a journal. That's been very helpful in my memoir writing given that my memory is failing.

Glazner: I noticed you had published a piece on suicide in rural areas.

Beeson: Yes. I spent most of my career in mental health, working on a variety of projects. Early on I worked in a state mental hospital and then spent some 25 years working for state government in health and human services. In fact, a strange aspect of this illness is that about a year ago I had a "flash back" to my work at the mental hospital and a particular patient there. Based upon that "memory flash back" I wrote my longest poem. I, also, wrote several poems about the farm crisis and they were published in the National Action Commission on the Mental Health of Rural Americans special report on the farm crisis. I did research on mental health in rural America and joined the National Association for Rural Mental Health (NARMH); eventually becoming president of that organization. And, I'm still involved with them and recently published an article (A New and Different Farm Crisis) in their journal.

Glazner : Here is a section from Beeson's long "memory flash back" poem, "Caring By the Numbers."

All the while she struggles,
"Help me!"
Withering in her bed,
"Help me!"
Fighting the straps,
 "Oh please God, help me."
Then I see them,
On her arm,

Etched in pale white skin,
Rumpled among the wrinkles,
Numbers tattooed there,
Faded blue-black numbers.

They don't mean anything
To me.
They just seem odd
And old,
Faded and tarnished,
Like her.

It's only later,
The next day,
When I learn the truth,
Comprehend, understand,
These are Auschwitz numbers,
Hitler's tattoo.

Glazner: What where the first signs you had Alzheimer's?

Beeson: The first signs for me were geographic. I couldn't picture where things were. I couldn't remember how to get to the airport. The first "Alzheimer's note" in my journal was this quote, "had another geographic lapse of memory, couldn't picture at all where the airport was, couldn't visualize it." That was in May of 2003.

Glazner: When did you start writing poetry?

Beeson: It was the early 1970s when I was in college. However, I didn't start writing poetry regularly until the early 1990s. I have written a lot of poems about my health experiences. I had heart by-pass surgery several years ago and wrote some 18 poems about that experience.

Glazner: I saw you had a piece on Cowboy Poetry in Nebraska Life.

Beeson: Yes, it's about the annual Cowboy Poetry festival they have in Valentine, Nebraska. However, for the magazine I mostly do photo essays.

Glazner: You have had many photographs published and I wanted to ask if you saw a connection between photography and poetry.

Beeson: Yes, I think there are connections in that in both you are trying to create images, through visual representation in photography and through the craft of words with poetry. Although, I guess it's not all that common to for someone to work in both photography and poetry.

Glazner: I found your poems to have striking images and to be concise and well crafted, almost as if they were a single photo, as opposed to a poem that moves through a series of images. For instance in your poem, "Here I Am," the image I have is of the plains and the openness of the plains. That openness comes back throughout your poems. It seems to me that there was a correlation between your poems and photography.

Beeson: Certainly it comes from the same person. I, however, think that photography is a little more opportunistic than poetry. You can craft the poem, simply reflecting, pausing and putting things down. In photography you have to get out, you are dependent of the circumstances on which you are in, e.g. available light.

Glazner: I see a connection between where you live, on the plains in Nebraska, and the images in your poetry, there is a shift between your experience and the landscape around you, that seems to give a photographic quality to the poems.

Beeson: I think there are some analogies between the experience of Alzheimer's and the Great Plains. There is vacantness of the plains and to this experience. It wasn't uncommon for the first settlers on the plains to get lost, not be able to find there way home. I think there is to some degree a connection between Alzheimer's and the actual layout of the Great Plains, the vast emptiness was disorienting and frightening to early pioneers just as Alzheimer's is to its victims.

HERE I AM
      —Peter G. Beeson

So I'm here,
Well, sort of here,
Mostly so,
But not quite all,
Here.

There is a detached
Vacantness,
A distant vagueness,
An absence
To my being.

Life's become a struggle,
The day-to-day a challenge,
The ordinary a novelty,
The routine an obstacle.

I long for the openness,
The emptiness,
The vastness
Of the Great Plains.

I long for a place
That matches my mind,
A place detached from memory,
An endless nothingness.

A place to lose oneself,
A place to disappear,
A place to become one
With earth and sky.

I AM NOT HERE
　　　—Peter G. Beeson

I'm not here,
No really,
You don't understand,
I'm not
Here.

Oh I know how it looks,
Like I am here;
Looks like it,
Seems like it,
But I'm not.

I'm not
Here,
Nor there,
Nor anywhere,
Really.

I float,
Suspended,
Waiting,
A cottonwood fairy
Launched by the breeze.

I'm out there,
Adrift, lost,
Cut loose,
Let go,
Gone.

THE WAY IT IS
        —Peter G. Beeson

Ya know,
It's just the way it is.
A fact
Like sunset or clouds,
Just there,
Come to roost,
Uninvited,
Like bad weather or drought,
A presence,
That grows day by day,
Like a rising tide
Or plague of grasshoppers,
Eating away
At your past
Consuming your future.

What's there to do?
How do you cope?
How long do you have?
Who do you tell?
How will it end?
What's next?
Can anything be done?
What should you do?
Is it inevitable?
How will it affect those you love?
Will you have to be cared for?
With what will you be left?
When will you be gone?
How much will you know?
How will it end?

STILL HERE

—Peter G. Beeson

I

I still know sunrise from sunset,
The difference between a rabbit and a squirrel,
A pine tree from a maple and that from an oak,
A rose from a daisy and that from a bluebonnet,
My left from my right and up from down,
My wife's face and my daughter's smile,
But for how long?

I can still find my way to work and home,
Put gas in the truck and wash dishes,
Mow the lawn and rake leaves,
Sweep the porch and feed the cat,
Pick up groceries and do bills,
Clean the toilet and do laundry,
But for how long?

I am still able to write,
Put things on paper,
Capture this or that,
Craft words and phrases,
Express hopes and fears,
Communicate,
But for how long?

II

But things do slip away, disappear,
Thoughts, memories, recollections, history,
Vanishing, drifting away, like dust in the wind.
I don't do what I said I would,
Wonder if I did it or not,
Forget this or that and them,
More and more.

Ordinary life,
The day to day,
The simple stuff,
The taken for granted,
The unthinking things,
The automatic,
Not like it use to be.

And so on and on I go,
Struggling from here to there,
To do this thing or that,
One little chore after another and another,
The ordinary becoming harder and harder,
The effort required greater and greater,
The sadness deeper and deeper.

III

Like a kite on a string,
Drifting aloft,
Only somewhat here,
Partially present,
Floating between the then and now,
Being pulled further and further away,
Disappearing into nothingness.

Like a fogged in ship,
Floating in a vast inland sea,
Devoid of anchor,
Absent of compass,
Only sometimes glimpsing the shore,
Only sometimes catching the wind,
Only sometimes.

Like a child lost on the prairie,
Wandering the great openness,
Unable to get my bearings,
Unable to find the stars,

Not knowing north or south, east or west,
Where I've been or where I'm going,
The way home.

IV

Fear and anger rise within me,
Alternating one with the other,
Holding me hostage,
Then suddenly fading away,
Leaving me vacant,
Empty,
Spent.

Sadness and loneliness
Pile one on top of another,
Such feelings of loss,
Helplessness,
Swell up within me,
Then fade into nothingness,
And I am just alone.

I want so to hold them tight,
Those that I love,
To feel their touch,
To have them close,
To never let them go,
To keep them next to me,
To not let me slip away.

The Lord is my shepherd, I shall not want. He makes me lie down in green pastures, He leads me beside quiet waters, He restores my soul. He guides me in paths of righteousness for His name's sake. Even though I walk through the valley of the shadow of death, I will fear no evil, for You are with me; Your rod and Your staff, they comfort me. You prepare a table before me in the presence of my enemies. You anoint my head with oil; my cup overflows. Surely goodness and love will follow me all the days of my life, and I will dwell in the house of the Lord forever.

COLOPHON

Set in *Mrs. Eaves*, designed by Zuzana Licko, distributed by Emigré. Mrs. Eaves is a revival type based on Baskerville, with a nod toward the warmth of the letterpress.

"Mrs. Eaves typeface is named after Sarah Eaves, the woman who became John Baskerville's wife. As Baskerville was setting up his printing and type business, Mrs. Eaves moved in with him as a live-in housekeeper, eventually becoming his wife after the death of her first husband, Mr. Eaves. Like the widows of Caslon, Bodoni, and the daughters of Fournier, Sarah similarly completed the printing of the unfinished volumes that John Baskerville left upon his death."

—ZUZANA LICKO

Titling is Mrs. Eaves ALLSMALL CAPS.

Book Design by Gary Mex Glazner.

Gary Mex Glazner makes his living as a poet. He is the director of the Alzheimer's Poetry Project. (APP) NBC's "Today," and NPR's "Weekend Edition," have featured segments on the APP. Harper Collins, W.W. Norton and Salon.com have published Glazner's work. Glazner is the editor of the "Word Art: Poetry Broadside Series," at the 400-year old Palace of the Governors Museum, where is learned to set type and run the old printing presses.

Photo by Reid Yalom

He is the author of "Ears on Fire: Snapshot Essays in a World of Poets," published on La Alameda Press, the book chronicles a year abroad in Asia and Europe meeting poets, working on translations and writing poems. Glazner is the host of "Poetry Talk," on KSFR in Santa Fe. He is the coach of Desert Academy's "Precision Poetry Drill Team," who were featured on NPR's "All Things Considered." Glazner's latest book is "How to Make a Living as a Poet," published by Soft Skull Press. Denise Kusel, of The Santa Fe New Mexican says, "Poet Gary Mex Glazner belies a mild-manner with an in-your-face delivery. He shouts. He postures. He's a madman, insisting you get it —all of it. Because he holds nothing back he's insightful and dangerous, as only a good poet can be."

SONNET 71

—William Shakespeare

No longer mourn for me when I am dead
Than you shall hear the surly sullen bell
Give warning to the world that I am fled
From this vile world, with vilest worms to dwell:
Nay, if you read this line, remember not
The hand that writ it; for I love you so,
That I in your sweet thoughts would be forgot,
If thinking on me then should make you woe.
O, if (I say) you look upon this verse,
When I perhaps compounded am with clay,
Do not so much as my poor name rehearse;
But let your love even with my life decay:
  Lest the wise world should look into your moan,
  And mock you with me after I am gone.